Saguaro
National Park

The Tucson Basin lies in the Sonoran Desert sixty miles north of the border between the United States and Mexico. It is surrounded by mountain ranges whose peaks stand as high as 9,400 feet above sea level, seven thousand feet above the basin itself. The city of Tucson lies cradled in the broad expanse between ranges. The Tucson Basin, like the 20 percent of the earth's land surface that is classified as desert, receives little moisture, about eleven inches a year.

The Sonoran Desert is one of the four distinct subdesert areas that are part of a larger, sprawling desert that cascades from Oregon and Idaho south well into Mexico. The three other components are the Great Basin, Mojave, and Chihuahuan deserts. Each of these has its own distinct look and feel: rugged, gullied, and flat, or perhaps sunken; as plantless as the moon, bristling with thorny shrubs and cactus, or somewhere in between; as hot as a griddle, or high and cold. Partly, these differences are brought about by rainfall—not the amount, for none of them get much, but by when it falls.

Teddy bear cholla backed by a valley thick with saguaro cactus and blossoming palo verde trees in the foothills of the Tucson Mountains.

Sunset light warms teddy bear cholla and Rincon Peak from the Tanque Verde Ridge trail in the Rincon Mountains.

The Sonoran Desert fairly bristles with plant life. There are dozens of varieties of cactus, short, tall, stout, delicate, tiny, as big as trees. Shrubs, grasses, trees, and flowers abound. This diversity is possible because the Sonoran Desert receives rain in both the winter and the summer. When the winter plants are dormant, the summer ones take over.

The Mighty Saguaro

Most prominent in the Sonoran panorama is the saguaro in its boundless variety of towering and many-armed shapes. In fact, this astonishing giant grows nowhere in the world but in the Sonoran Desert, and only in portions of the Sonoran Desert at that. The Tucson Basin is situated near the desert's eastern boundary and the habitat limit of this spectacular symbol of the American Southwest. Not nearly as widespread as the sets of cowboy movies would have us believe, the saguaro occupies a limited range: elevations between sea level and 4,500 feet, with well-drained rocky soils and temperatures that do not remain below freezing for more than twenty hours or so. Summer temperatures in the Sonoran Desert can reach 120 degrees Fahrenheit. Winter temperatures seldom fall below freezing for more than a day at a time.

Within the Tucson Basin, which provides the ideal conditions for sustaining dense stands of saguaro cactus, is Saguaro National Park, established in 1933 to preserve and protect this striking Sonoran Desert dweller, its habitat, and the other life forms within it. The park, made up of two districts, contains mountains as well as desert, the peaks of the former providing homes for many plants and animals that require cooler, wetter environments. The Rincon Mountain District covers 104 square miles on the eastern edge of Tucson, and twenty-five miles to the west is the Tucson Mountain District, encompassing thirty-nine square miles. The two districts are quite distinct, and it is well worth the time to explore the trails and roads of each to gain a sense of its uniqueness.

Water makes up 75 to 95 percent of the saguaro's weight, its pleats contracting as it survives through long periods without rain and expanding as it soaks up moisture when it becomes available.

The Rincon Mountain District contains most of the Rincon Mountain Range. The lower elevations are home to saguaros and other desert scrub community plants. As the land rises to 8,666 feet in elevation at the summit of Mica Mountain, desert scrub gives way to desert grassland, which melds into oak woodland, then to pine forest. On the very highest peaks of this "island in the desert" mixed conifers find niches on north-facing slopes. Exposed metamorphic rock—gneiss and schist—hints at the geologic history of the mountains.

The Tucson Mountain District presents a very different aspect. The elevation is generally lower, and the saguaro stands are much more dense. They march from the sandy expanse of the Avra Valley up the alluvial slopes and onto the jagged volcanic mountains to near the 4,687-foot crest of the Tucson Mountains.

The Sonoran Desert landscape has its own perfectly evolved beauty. The rocky terrain is furrowed with washes eroded by the downpours of sudden rainstorms. Gravelly flats shimmer in the blinding sunlight. Mountains, dark and rugged, rise in the distance. The vista is filled with an astonishing assortment of the desert's 2,700 known plant species.

Saguaros, like many desert plants, grow excruciatingly slowly. We can estimate that a forty-foot-tall individual is about 150 years old. Growth is slowest at the seedling stage, with the cactus taking perhaps five years to become one inch tall. Arm buds appear after about seventy-five years. Many saguaros now standing in the cactus forest germinated in the mid-1800s.

To survive their early years, saguaro seedlings must be sheltered from the elements, whether it be under the canopy of other plants or in the crevices of rocky outcrops. Sometimes saguaro seeds are deposited in droppings of birds roosting on the branches of larger shrubs and trees. The tiny seedlings, sheltered by these "nurse plants," shaded from the blistering summer sun, blanketed on a freezing winter night, perhaps hidden from hugry woodrats, have a chance to get a start on life.

TOP: Winter storm runoff cascades down metamorphic gneiss near the Rincon Mountain District's Cactus Forest Drive.
BOTTOM: Saguaro and ironwood in bloom

Saguaros' root systems are wide-reaching and shallow, allowing quick absorption of moisture. The downside of this arrangement is that they are easily blown over when the ground becomes saturated and soft. Plants growing on rocky areas can anchor their roots more effectively and lessen the danger of toppling over.

Water makes up 75 to 95 percent of the saguaro's weight, its pleats contracting as it survives through long periods without rain and expanding as it soaks up moisture when it becomes available. This ability to store large quan-

tities of water, and adaptations such as their waxy coating, which prevents evaporation, enable saguaros to thrive in a harsh environment.

The substantial mass of a saguaro provides insulation, and the interior remains much cooler than the outside temperature. The Gila woodpecker and the gilded flicker peck large cavities into the flesh of the saguaro, and the dark coolness provides a home for them and their offspring. This invasion usually does not seriously injure the plant, which forms a woody layer, or scab, over the wound to prevent loss of moisture. After the original occupant abandons the nest, other birds quickly move in. Many types of insects also use the vacated holes. Woody cavity linings, or "boots" as they are called because of their typical shape, can be found among the remains of dead and decomposing plants.

Doves, as well as larger birds such as red-tailed hawks and great horned owls, may build their nests on, rather than in, the saguaro. They can be seen settled in the joint of an arm.

In May and June, the saguaro's primary flowering months, large, white, waxy flowers create glorious crowns on the tips of stems and arms. Blooms are present for about a month, as buds open a few at a time.

Individual flowers have one night of glorious bloom, from after sunset until mid-morning of the following day, before their petals close and turn brown, and seeds begin to develop within the ovary. Lesser long-nosed bats and white-winged doves rely heavily on the nectar held deep within the flower. As these animals extract the nectar, their heads become dusted with pollen, which is then deposited in the next flower as feeding progresses. Because saguaro pollen is heavy and not easily windborne, visits by animals are essential for cross-pollination.

During the following month, the fruits ripen and turn crimson. Rains don't begin until July, but the sweet, juicy fruits, packed with small black seeds, provide moisture and nourishment for many animals in the intense, dry heat of June. Birds perch atop the saguaro and feast. Fruit that falls to the ground is quickly devoured by coyotes, foxes, skunks, javelinas, squirrels, woodrats, and other desert creatures. Of the approximately two thousand seeds contained in each fruit, only a few will germinate, and only a small percentage of those will survive animal depredation and the elements to reach maturity.

For unknown reasons, the stem of a saguaro will sometimes grow in an unusual shape. This cristate, or crested, development does not interfere with flower or fruit production.

Lightning, powerful winds, harsh winter freezes and the resulting rotting of dead tissue kill saguaros, and their woody ribs stand or lie on the desert floor until they are consumed by termites or decay and return to the soil.

Other cacti are abundant in the Sonoran Desert as well. Food and lodging for desert animals are provided by fishhook barrels, prickly pears, pincushions,

OPPOSITE: (Clockwise) White-winged dove, cactus wren, Gambel's quail, greater roadrunner, elf owl

TOP: Ocotillo flowers

BOTTOM: Desert globemallow

TOP: Desert tarantula
CENTER: Gila monster
BOTTOM: Western diamondback rattlesnake

hedgehogs, and many other varieties of cactus. Cholla's tiny barbed spines attach to skin or clothing at the slightest touch. Birds, however, build nests and raise young in this unlikely nursery, and the raucous warning call of the cactus wren may signal the threat of a snake winding its way into the cholla's branches looking for a meal.

Not every plant that grows in this desert is a cactus, however. Cacti have regularly spaced areoles—roundish raised or depressed areas—from which spines and branches usually originate. Agave, sotol, bear grass, and ocotillo are among the plants seen in the Sonoran Desert that do not have areoles and are not cacti.

Desert Adaptations

All plants inhabiting the desert have undergone adaptations that enable them to survive. When it gets too hot and dry, some plants simply die off. But before they do, they scatter their seeds, which grow in another season. These are the annuals, and in the Sonoran Desert there are summer and winter groups.

Some plants become dormant until conditions improve. Ocotillo, abundant in the park, is a good example of this adaptation. When it rains, ocotillos quickly sprout leaves; when it becomes dry, the leaves fall. This cycle can happen many times in one year. Most desert plants, including cactus, have developed water conservation strategies. Water is stored in their roots and stems, and the waxy coating on stems and leaves minimizes evaporation. Some varieties of shrubs and trees, in order to reduce transpiration, have no leaves, or only tiny ones. The palo verde tree has green trunks and branches, where photosynthesis or food manufacturing takes place.

Plants with leaves are desert adapted, too. The mesquite's leaflets fold together when stressed by drought, to conserve whatever minute quantities of water remain. When leaves are present on desert plants, they are usually small and may be leathery, hairy, waxy, or varnished. They may be grayish in color to reflect the sun, or perhaps they may grow at an angle that avoids their being struck directly by the sun's rays.

Adaptation takes place below the ground as well as above, and root systems have made important adjustments to desert life. Some plants, like the mesquite tree, send down tremendously long roots to take advantage of groundwater. Most cactus root systems are extensive but close to the surface, so that they rapidly soak up moisture from every small rainfall. Some plant species have both deep and surface roots.

During the heat of the day most large desert mammals—mule deer, javelina, coyote, and gray and kit foxes—seek out the relatively cool shade of trees. The pocket mouse, antelope ground squirrel, kangaroo rat, and other abundant rodents excavate burrows in which they wait out the heat. Piles of plant debris deposited in washes and gullies by fast-running water from sudden rainstorms make excellent shelter for many small creatures. Animals may be active during the day, but when the sun drops low in the sky, activity picks up as many more emerge to hunt, browse, and go about their nocturnal business. The yips and howls of coyotes, chirps of crickets, calls of owls, and soft scurrying of small creatures fill the darkness.

Even on the hottest of summer days, desert lizards are in evidence. Reptiles regulate their body temperature by moving from shade to sun to shade. Lizards run with their bodies held high above the hot soil; some even run on their hind legs.

The Sonoran Desert is home to a variety of snakes, including the western diamondback rattlesnake, but they are not commonly seen. They escape the cold of winter and the heat of summer days by retreating to underground rodent holes. When they are out and about, their protective coloring is such a perfect match to the background of rocks and splotches of shade and light that they often go unnoticed.

The sound of the Sonoran Desert is one of its most memorable aspects. Cool mornings and late afternoons are a cacophony of melodies, squawks, screeches, coos, and whistles of birds. There are multitudes of species at home here. The soaring hawk, the busy, rasping cactus wren, the white-winged dove, and the jewel-like hummingbird, represent just the tip of the avian iceberg.

Above the Saguaros

Saguaro National Park extends above the desert scrub community. One hundred miles of hiking trails wind through the Rincon Mountains, passing through six life zones. The 6,000-foot elevation change corresponds climatologically to the change in latitude from northern Mexico to southern Canada. With rising elevation, mosses and ferns become more common. Plants with long, fleshy leaves—sotol, agave, and yucca—appear. The oak woodland appears at about 4,000 feet above sea level, then pines predominate, and at 8,000 feet the mixed conifer forest is reached.

As the vegetation changes with elevation, so do the animals. Black bears, white-tailed deer, and gray squirrels seldom venture down into the desert. There are eleven kinds of birds that range no lower than the 4,000-foot oak woodland.

The Rincon Mountain District includes the highest mountains in the park. Their tilting strata are witness to the uplift about twenty million years ago that raised them to their present height. The tremendous forces and movements involved in this upheaval resulted in the metamorphosis of the outer granite into a shell of gneiss and schist that makes up much of the surface of the Rincons today.

TOP: Javelina
CENTER: Kit fox
BOTTOM: Bobcat

Between 10,000 and 1,700 years ago, nomadic hunter-gatherers established base camps along major drainage systems in the Rincon Mountains. Their hunting and food preparation tools are found in both districts of Saguaro National Park.

The geology of the Tucson Mountains differs from that of the Rincons. This range is made up of younger sedimentary, intrusive, and volcanic rocks. Recent research has revealed a complex but fascinating geologic history. Enormous volcanoes formed on the surface above the masses of molten magma that would later form the cores of the Santa Catalina and Rincon mountains. Occasional volcanic explosions would cause calderas, vast bowl-shaped collapses, into which would tumble older surrounding rockbeds and layers of ash from continuing eruptions. One of these calderas was situated above the rocks of today's Santa Catalina Mountains, which were not yet uplifted to their present elevation. The mass of the caldera rim and its collection of internal deposits separated from the Santa Catalina core magma along nearly horizontal detachment faults, and over the course of millions of years inched westward to become the Tucson Mountains. Near the Red Hills Visitor Center of the Tucson Mountain District the red sandstone is composed of materials eroded from the volcanic highlands to the east and deposited as sediments on the floodplain of an ancient sea.

Desert Home

The earliest human habitation of the Tucson area dates to about 11,500 years ago when mammoth, bison, and other large mammals foraged among plants of a cooler, wetter Pleistocene climate. Small groups of indigenous people hunted with stone-tipped spears and gathered food along marshy shores of shallow lakes and streams. Around 10,000 years ago, as the climate began to warm and dry, the vegetation changed, and large Pleistocene mammals became extinct.

Between 10,000 and 1,700 years ago, nomadic hunter-gatherers established base camps along major drainage systems in the Rincon Mountains. Their hunting and food preparation tools are found in both districts of Saguaro National Park.

By 1,700 years ago the Hohokam culture, which probably evolved from the earlier hunter-gatherers, developed in southern Arizona. The Hohokam lived in villages of pithouses: structures of mud applied to wooden frameworks, with floors a foot or so below the ground surface. Using rock terraces and canals to direct rainwater to crops, they raised corn, beans, squash, and cotton on desert floodplains. Hohokam agricultural sites are found in the Rincon Mountain District.

In both districts of the park impressive petroglyphs and pictographs are found, probably left by Hohokam farmers 700 to 1,300 years ago. The Hohokam pecked onto rock surfaces human figures, lizards, large animals, turtles, snakes, birds, and insects. In Saguaro National Park, abstract elements—sunbursts, wavy lines, and mazes—are found much more often than representational figures. Circles—large and small, concentric, joined, in clusters, and in other combinations—are common. Hohokam petroglyph sites display spirals more often than do other southwestern locations.

The Next Immigrants

About 500 years ago most Hohokam sites were abandoned. Archeologists speculate that farming conditions may have deteriorated as the climate changed, or there may have been intergroup war or migration out of the area. When the Spanish entered the Tucson area in the late 1600s, groups of Piman speaking people were living there. Their connection to the Hohokam is not known, though legends and some similarities to the Hohokam lifestyle argue for a close association.

European contact came first with the Jesuit missionaries, led by Padre Eusebio Kino in the late 1600s; Spanish soldiers soon followed, and eventually

The Tohono O'odham

The use of the saguaro cactus for food and building material provides a tie between the modern Tohono O'odham and the prehistoric occupants of this desert. Today, the summer saguaro fruit harvest provides a tantalizing glimpse into history. In summer, Tohono O'odham families travel to their traditional campsites for a month's labor under the hot June sun. Early each morning they venture out from their ramadas, which are traditionally made of saguaro ribs, carrying long saguaro-rib poles. These they use to knock down the ripe fruit from high up on the tips of the cactus's trunk and arms. They bring back buckets of the juicy red fruit, and for the next few hours the day's harvest is boiled in large kettles over wood fires. The pulp is removed and seeds are strained to be dried and eaten later. The crimson syrup is preserved in jars and will be enjoyed for months to come.

TOP: The foothills of the Rincon Mountain District
BOTTOM: Hohokam petroglyphs on Signal Hill, Safford and Panther peaks in the background

Saguaro and prickly pear cactus

ranchers and farmers. As westward expansion proceeded, Tucson's population grew, and by the late 1800s there was ranching and farming in the area that is now the Rincon Mountain District. Though the area was designated a national monument in 1933, grazing permits allowed cattle to remain among the giant cactus for another four decades. By the time federal policies ended grazing in the 1970s, heavy grazing had denuded the land. It wasn't until the mid-1980s that the last feral cattle were removed.

Grazing and trampling were not the only impacts. By the time the monument was established, nearly every mesquite tree had been taken from the western portion of the Rincon district to be used for fuel or fence posts. Woodcutters removed the trees that acted as nurse plants to young saguaros. Thieves removed saguaros and other cactuses to be replanted in city yards.

Meanwhile, in the Tucson Mountains to the west, miners began to prospect for silver, gold, and copper. The tunnels and shafts produced little ore. Because there was little settlement, grazing, or woodcutting in this dry and rocky terrain, the vegetation remained relatively unchanged. The Tucson Mountain District was added to the monument in 1961, and in 1994 Congress declared Saguaro National Monument a national park.

Fragile Giants

For all their robust appearance, saguaros are quite fragile. Prolonged cold presents a great danger to these titans. February 1939 brought the coldest period ever recorded; temperatures fell to twenty-five degrees Fahrenheit and remained there for several hours.

Before long soft-rot began to invade the saguaros and spread rapidly through the forest. In 1941 the National Park Service, in efforts to stop the spread, attempted to remove and bury affected portions or whole plants when necessary. The saguaro population continued to ebb and the specter of saguaro extinction loomed before the scientific community.

As research continued, it was discovered that some plants seemed unable to create a callus around attacking bacteria and thereby seal them off from healthy tissue. Scientists drew a correlation between wounds and rot. Perhaps, they theorized, the saguaros had become weakened by the freeze and were unable to fend off the bacteria.

Ecologist Dr. Charles Lowe and his student, Warren Steenbergh, undertook extensive research on saguaro rot. Their studies focused on shifts in saguaro population densities in conjunction with changes in climate and solar radiation.

They pointed out that this particular saguaro forest had not experienced freezes for several decades before 1939 and, therefore, had not been culled of old and weak individuals. They held that the bacterial rot was not the cause of the die-off, but instead was attacking already damaged plants.

Nature has taught federal resource managers some graphic lessons about environmental fluctuations. There is a place for fire, wind, cold, heat, and

Sonoran Desert Wildflowers

The desert in bloom is a wonderful sight to behold. In a feast for the eyes, wide expanses of owl's clover, desert marigold, purple lupine, and Mexican poppies blossom.

But why do flowers appear some years and not others? Most desert wildflowers are annuals so they must grow from seeds sown from previous years. For those seeds to germinate, winter temperatures need to be cool, but not too cool. A freeze at just the wrong time will halt a good bloom.

Another important factor is moisture. The winter rains, which hopefully dampen this desert between October and February, help to bring out the brilliant February through April blooms.

The proper combination of moisture and temperature is an important factor in protecting the seeds for years to come. Seeds only germinate when all the requirements are met. This way when they do sprout, they'll be able to grow to maturity and produce more seed, continuing the cycle.